The Ministry of the Altar Server

CAROLINE M. THOMAS

RESOURCE PUBLICATIONS, INC.
San Jose, California
www.rpinet.com

Reprint Department
Resource Publications, Inc.
160 E. Virginia Street, #170
San Jose, CA 95112
(408) 286-8505
(408) 287-8748 fax
www.rpinet.com

Library of Congress Cataloging-in-Publication Data

Thomas, Caroline M., 1943-
The ministry of the altar server / Caroline M. Thomas.
p. cm.
ISBN-13: 978-0-89390-712-9 (pbk.)
ISBN-10: 0-89390-712-X (pbk.)
1. Acolytes--Catholic Church. I. Title.
BX1915.T46 2012
264'.02--dc23

2012001896

Printed in the United States of America
12 13 14 15 16 | 5 4 3 2 1

Cover illustration: Lisa Lentz
Illustrations: Lisa Lentz
Design and production: Kenneth Guentert, The Publishing Pro, LLC
Copyeditor: Barbara Mellen

Contents

Introduction

Congratulations! You've decided to become an altar server in your parish. There are many reasons young people decide to become servers. Do you know why you made that choice? Perhaps you have an older family member who served at Mass and you thought you'd like to do what they did. Or maybe you see the servers up front every week and decided that it looked like a fun or "cool" thing to do.

Regardless of your reason for making the decision, there will be some consequences. One is that you will develop a new understanding of the Mass since you will become actively involved in a new way. The new understanding of the Mass and the added active role will make being at Mass more interesting and meaningful for you.

Another result of your decision is that you will be helpful during Mass. You can help make everything flow more smoothly. This will make the Mass a better and more prayerful experience for everyone.

So let's talk about what your decision will mean for you.

Service at the Altar Is a Ministry

Regardless of what brought you to become involved as an altar server, it is important to understand what it means. The name "server" tells you. The word indicates that you will be providing a service. Whom will you serve?

Sometimes people think that altar servers are there to serve the priest. Actually their function is to help the priest serve the people in the assembly. Those people are necessary. Without them, there would be no job for any of the ministers. There would be no one to serve.

Service to the people of the assembly is very important. The assembly is Christ's presence in the world. We call it the Body of Christ. Vatican Council II made a point of telling us that the people gathered in the assembly are one of the primary ways that Christ is present. So in serving them, you are also serving Christ.

The assembly, which has been called by God to gather for worship, is the reason the rest of the ministries exist. The assembly includes you. And the priest. And the other ministers. Everyone has been called by God to assemble to celebrate the Mass. We all serve one another.

The other word for service is "ministry." In fact, we will use that word most of the time in referring to your role during the Mass. We think of priests as being ministers. So are readers and greeters and ushers and musicians and all who serve God's people assembled for worship. Ministry means service, but it is a kind of specialized service. Any time we do something for someone else, it can be called service. When we call it a ministry, we imply a religious aspect to what we do. Ministry could be called, "service in God's name."

How do you serve the people gathered for worship? There is not much that you do to or for them directly. By assisting the priest, holding things for him and bringing him things he needs, you help the Mass to flow more smoothly and therefore to be more prayerful for the people who attend.

For this reason it is important to be attentive and ready to move when it is time to bring a book, carry a candle, or whatever is needed. If there is a delay and the priest, whom we call a presider in his role at Mass, has to turn around to cue you, it is a distraction to the people and can pull them from their prayer. This prayer is what all those who minister are supposed to encourage and make possible. Anything that distracts from it is to be avoided. It robs the people of their opportunity to relate to God during this special time that we call "liturgy."

The word "liturgy" is loosely translated as "the work of the people." So they need to be able to do it. They need to be able to focus on it and not be distracted. When they do their work, they are ministering to one another and to all who are present, including you. They are able to be open to God's love and grace. If they are distracted, they lose this opportunity.

How to Be Present during Mass

What are some of the ways that you can accomplish this ministry to assist people in prayer and not distract them?

1. Use good posture. Stand, sit, and kneel up straight. Do not slouch. Be a good example by showing reverence and attentiveness in the way you stand, sit, or kneel. Keep your hands folded or quietly in your lap or on your knees. If the community is singing, hold a songbook or hymnal so you can sing along. If you do not yet have the prayers memorized, pick up a missalette, or whatever is provided for you, so you can say the prayers with everyone else and give a good example.

2. Be reverent. When you move, move slowly and deliberately. If you are sitting, remain still and attentive. If you wiggle, people will notice it and be distracted. It is difficult to sit still, but important that you do so. Stretching and yawning will tell people that you are bored. This is not the message you wish to give, and it will pull people away from their prayer or listening. There should be no talking. Before Mass starts it should be decided who will do what. There should be no need for discussion during the liturgy.

I recently attended Mass in a parish where the altar servers were very well trained. They sat very still with their hands on their knees. When they stood, they folded their hands in a prayer position and stood up straight and still. There was no distraction on the part of the servers. They were attentive to the action of the liturgy and participated in it. They were serious and reverent whether they were processing or simply in their seats. Not only did it not detract from the action of the liturgy, it contributed to it and set a good example for the assembly.

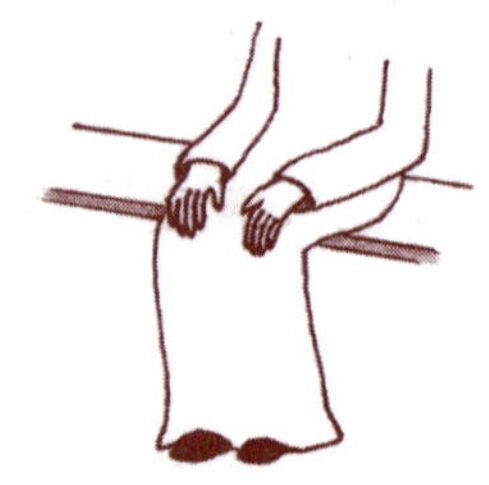

Remember that you are in a sacred space. You will act differently here from how you act in other places. You will move more slowly and quietly. You are in a place of prayer. Remember that all your actions are prayers. If you have that attitude of prayerfulness when you serve, your actions will naturally be appropriate.

3. Know your part. Be ready to move when it is your turn. Liturgy needs to flow smoothly. When the presider says, “Let us pray,” go to hold the book for him without delay. If he needs to turn to look at you or in some way remind you that it is time to move, the people will be distracted from what they have been asked to do, which is to make their own prayers in their hearts. Any time directions have to be given in liturgy, it detracts from the prayerfulness.

   Liturgy is a ritual action. Rituals are repeated actions that are consistently the same. That means that people know what to do, or what to expect. They don’t have to think about it. The predictable repetition contributes to a comfortable familiarity. That is why when the priest says "The Lord be with you," the people know what to say. They have learned their response. They don't have to think about it. People know when to sit or stand or kneel, because it is the same every time. When visiting another parish where things are done a little differently, you notice that it is harder to focus on prayer when one needs to watch to see when people are going to kneel or stand.

Sometimes parts of the ritual are changed in order to draw attention to them. For example, if a parish does not usually sing the "Lord, have mercy," singing it during a special season like Lent, focuses on the penitential aspect of that season. Just remember that it is important that you do your part of the ritual so that you do not draw attention to yourself.

4. Move slowly. Nothing attracts attention as quickly as a swift movement. Frequently servers (and others) move quickly because they think that people will be less likely to see them. The opposite is true. Moving slowly and reverently rarely draws attention. One quick movement draws the eye, and that is what you want to avoid. Even if you make a mistake, keep your movements slow and it may be that no one will even notice the mistake. If you move quickly, for sure they will notice it.

5. Move gracefully. As ministers you serve in Christ's name. What you do is important and valuable. Your posture and movements should show this. They should be deliberate, purposeful, and graceful. There should be pride in what

you do. This is not a pride in yourself, but a pride in the value of what you are doing. This should make you want to do it as well as possible. There should be a calmness about you. For example, when processing in at the beginning of Mass, your pace should be slow and graceful. Not unnaturally slow, but reverently slow.

6. Be a good example. In most church buildings the people can see the altar servers all during the Mass. It is important that the servers participate in the Mass as members of the assembly, doing what the people are doing, unless they are doing something specifically in their role as servers. The servers sing the hymns and acclamations. They listen to the readings and the homily. They pray the same prayers as the people. They are an example of what the people are to do. It may be that you decided to become a server because you saw someone else do it. Your good example may cause someone else to become a server.

Expectations

Once you have signed up to be an altar server, some things will be expected of you.

You will be expected to attend the training sessions. This is extremely important in order to learn what to do and to become comfortable in doing it. You will become comfortable when you are sure that you know what to do and when to do it. If there is anything you do not understand, do not be afraid to ask for an explanation. Probably others do not understand either, but may be too shy to ask. If there is something you did not hear, be sure to ask for it to be repeated. You don't want to miss anything that you will need to know.

Even things that seem simple, like lighting candles, need to be practiced. There are techniques to everything that make the actions easier and more graceful. Also, it is surprising how much more difficult some of these things seem when you are at Mass in front of the assembly.

When there are practices or "walk-throughs," ask to do it as many times as you need to feel comfortable and secure in what you are doing. Of course you will feel a little nervous the first few times. Usually parishes schedule experienced servers with the new ones to give them confidence and to assist them if they get confused or nervous.

You will be expected to show up to serve when you are scheduled. Be sure to check the schedule so that you know when you are assigned to serve. If, for some reason, you are unable to serve at the scheduled time, because your family will be out of town for example, get a substitute or switch times with someone as soon as possible. Then let the scheduler know that the change has been made to the schedule. If the scheduler will be the one to get a substitute, let the scheduler know about the needed change as soon as possible.

Some parishes ask the servers to sign themselves up for the times they are available. Don't wait until the last minutes, but sign up as soon as the signup sheet becomes available. (This will also give you the best choice of times to serve.)

You will be expected to look ready for Sunday Mass when you arrive. This means you will be clean and neat. Most parishes provide garments to put on over your clothes. These are called albs. Traditionally albs are white garments that represent our baptism. It is from your baptism that you receive the right and the responsibility to minister. Sometimes the albs are an "off-white" so they don't show dirt as easily.

The servers in some parishes wear cassocks and surplices instead of albs. The cassocks are long black or sometimes red garments. Over them is a white loose fitting short garment called the surplice. These are a traditional vestment for altar servers.

Someone, maybe one of the mothers, will be responsible for laundering these vestments. You can show your appreciation for the work that they do by taking good care of them. For one thing, when you are finished with serving, hang the garment up neatly on a hanger. Fasten the button, snap, zipper, or tie so that it will not slide off the hanger. Not only does this show appreciation to whoever cleans the vestments, it is also a sign of respect and consideration for the next server who will use them.

Some clothes show under the albs or cassocks. They should look appropriate for Sunday Mass. For example, pant legs should not be frayed. Shoes always show. If you have them, you should wear dress shoes so they look like they fit appropriately with the alb. If all you have is tennis shoes, wear the nicest and cleanest ones you have. People notice these things. Dressing nicely is respectful of the people you serve and of the ministry in which you serve.

The garments for Mass come in different sizes. Be sure to find out which size fits you so that it looks good and doesn't trip you because it is too long. That would be a distraction! Also, besides embarrassing you, it might cause something to be spilled or broken. So always make sure that you have the correct size. If a cincture (a tied belt that looks like a cord) is used with the alb, make certain that it is tied correctly and that all looks neat. It need not be too tight, but should be snug enough that it doesn't look like it will fall off. It will make the alb a little shorter, so that should be considered when selecting the size.

One Ministry among Many

The altar server ministers alongside the other liturgical ministers and interacts with them. Mass is a community affair. All are there to serve one another. Some interactions are more obvious than others.

The interaction with the priest presider is very obvious, since most of what you do will be to help him in his role as a leader of the people's prayer. You know that you will be bringing the book over to him and holding it for him while he reads from it. This enables him to be more present to the people in the assembly and to have his hands free for a prayer posture. At the same time that he is leading the people's prayer, he is leading yours as well. Your job, whether or not you are holding a book for him, is to pray with him as a member of the assembly. You will say the "Amen" and other prayers with them.

The members of the assembly are the primary music ministers. The song is their responsibility. You are part of that. The musicians also minister as they lead the assembly in song. Sometimes in your role as an altar server you can't always sing unless you have the song memorized, because your hands are occupied with holding other things instead of the songbook. However, when you have finished your serving task and go back to your seat, pick up the songbook and join the community's song. This is another way to serve the community, through your example of song, through your prayer in singing it (the hymns are sung prayers), and through supporting the musicians' leadership through your participation. Even the presiders are supposed to participate in the singing as members of the assembly. During the community's song, the musicians are leading the assembly's prayer.

You minister to the readers by listening attentively when they proclaim God's word. Many presiders show that they also are being receptive to this ministry by turning in their chair and looking at the reader. This models what the congregation should be doing. This attentiveness on the part of all helps the readers to do their part better. It is much easier to proclaim the readings if it is obvious that people are listening. For your part you receive their ministry in the form of God's word proclaimed to you. Listen carefully. Even if you have heard this reading before, you may hear something new if you are listening for what God wants to tell you this day.

This is also true for the presiders and deacons when they proclaim the Gospel. It is the same kind of interaction between reader and listener. Once again, your example to the community is important. And it is VERY important that you do nothing that would distract them from hearing God's word spoken to them. It would be a shame if they (or you) missed it.

Those who distribute Holy Communion (ordained or lay) obviously minister to you by giving you Christ's Body and Blood in the consecrated bread and wine. You minister to them by helping to get the cups and dishes ready and on the altar. You also minister to them by receiving Holy Communion from them in a reverent and graceful manner. Those whom they serve minister to them in return.

The ushers, who tend to the physical aspects of the building, serve you also. They may be the ones responsible for making sure the heating or air conditioning is on to keep a comfortable temperature in the building. The greeters welcome people and help to make them feel comfortable in praying and singing with this community. They make it easier for the members of the assembly to do their ministry at the liturgy. You minister to the ushers and greeters as you do to all the other members of the community.

Finally, and perhaps most important, are the members of the assembly. We have mentioned many ways that you minister to them by making the Mass more prayerful and by being good examples in prayer and song and attentive reverence. All members of the assembly, including you, minister to one another through prayer, and through the witness of faith to one another. It is much easier to be strong in faith, even in difficult times, when we are supported by one another's faith witness.

New Names to Learn

As you train to become an altar server, there are a lot of new words to learn; names of things that you may not have heard before, even though you have seen them at Mass.

Parts of the Church Building

Nave: The main body of the church where the assembly is seated.

Sacristy: The area, usually in the front of the church building near the sanctuary, where the priest gets ready for Mass. The books, vestments, and sacred vessels are stored there.

Sanctuary: The part of the church building around the altar. Usually the ambo and presider's chair are in the sanctuary. In most churches the altar servers are also seated there.

Vestibule: The entrance area to the church building between the outside doors and the inside doors. Sometimes this is called the narthex.

Special Names for People

Acolyte: One who serves at the altar. These can be adults as well as young people. Usually it is used as another name for altar server. At one time a rite of ordination was necessary in order to become an acolyte.

Deacon: An ordained minister whose special role in the liturgy is to read the gospel and preach the homily. He also invites many of the assembly's responses, for example at the sign of peace. Deacons can baptize, preside at burials, and witness at weddings.

Presider: The person who leads (presides at) the people's prayer. Most often it refers to the priest's role at Mass.

Sacristan: A person who sets up for Mass and other liturgical celebrations. He or she is responsible for the items in the sacristy. Not every parish has a separate individual for this function.

Garments

Alb: A baptismal garment, long, white—or sometimes off-white—as a reminder of baptism. The altar servers frequently wear albs, although they may wear other vestments. The priest wears an alb under his chasuble, and sometimes with just a stole when he is not celebrating Mass.

Amice: A rectangular piece of white fabric with ties attached to be worn over the shoulders and around the neck of the priest when he is dressed for Mass. The amice covers the collar of his street clothes when he wears his vestments. Not all priests use them.

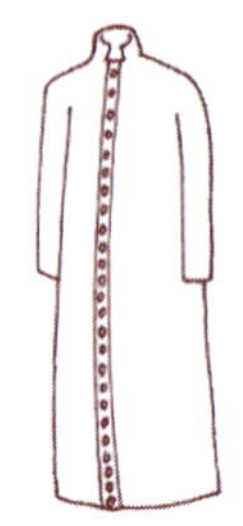

Cassock: A long close-fitting black (or sometimes red) robe that buttons down the front. Some priests wear them as daily attire. Some altar servers use them with a white surplice over the top part. Monsignors wear ones that are a magenta color.

Chasuble: A sleeveless outer vestment worn by the priest at Mass. It is in the color of the season or the feast, such as violet for Lent or white for Easter. Some styles look similar to a poncho.

Cincture: A long woven cord, usually out of a soft cotton, which fastens around the waist of an alb.

Cope: A long cape worn for processions, benediction, and other events other than Mass. It usually fastens in front with a single clasp.

Humeral Veil: A long cloth draped over the shoulders of the celebrant when carrying the Blessed Sacrament in procession, either in a monstrance, or on Holy Thursday in a ciborium.

Stole: A long strip of fabric that is placed around the neck of a priest with the two ends hanging down the front. It is a symbol of ordination and matches the chasuble in color. Depending on the style, it can be worn over or under the chasuble. The deacon wears a stole, but the deacon's stole drapes across the left shoulder and is fastened below the waist on the right side.

Surplice: A loose-fitting, short white tunic worn over a cassock.

Vestments: Special articles of clothing worn by ministers for church worship services.

Church Furnishings

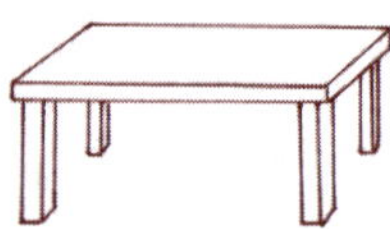

Altar: A primary symbol in the church building. It represents Christ's body. This is why we bow when we cross in front of it.

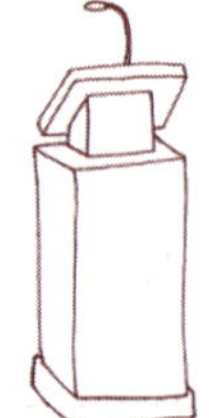

Ambo: The place from which the word of God is proclaimed. The prayers of the faithful are also read from the ambo. It has sometimes been called a pulpit or lectern. It is one of the primary symbols in a Catholic Church.

Ambry: The location of the holy oils. This can be a cabinet or shelf, or individual stands.

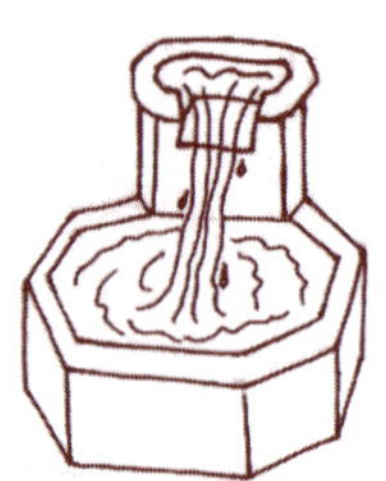

Baptismal Font: The third of the primary symbols in a Catholic Church. This holds the holy water that will be used to baptize those coming into the Catholic faith. Ideally this is located near the front entrance to the church building to symbolize that we come into the church through the waters of baptism. Those entering bless themselves with the water from it.

Holy Water Fonts: These remind us of the baptismal font. They are found at the entrance to many churches and contain holy water so those entering the building can bless themselves as a reminder of their baptism. They are used if the baptismal font is not available at the entrance.

Credence Table: A table in the church to hold items that will be used during the service.

Gifts Table: A specific credence table normally located in the back of the church. It holds the bread and wine that will be brought up during the presentation of gifts time during Mass, just after the collection.

Presider's Chair: The chair that the priest uses at Mass and from which he leads some of the prayers.

Sanctuary Lamp: A candle, usually enclosed in glass, which burns in a Catholic Church to let people know that the Blessed Sacrament is present in the tabernacle. Sometimes it is referred to as a "presence lamp" because it indicates Christ's presence in the tabernacle.

Tabernacle: A receptacle, usually made from metal, with a door on the front. It holds the consecrated hosts left over from Mass so that they can be taken to the sick and also used for adoration.

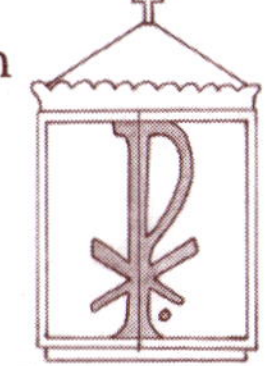

Books

Book of Blessings: Contains blessings for various occasions, people, places, and items.

The Book of the Gospels: Contains the Gospel readings for Sundays, solemnities, feasts of the Lord, and some ritual Masses.

Lectionary (Four Volumes): Contains all the readings for Mass. It includes the responsorial psalm and the alleluia verse even though these are usually sung. The first volume is for Sundays, feasts, and solemnities. The other three are for various weekday Masses.

Rite Books: Books that are used for special occasions.

Rite of Baptism for Children: Used when children are baptized.

Rite of Marriage: Used for weddings.

Rite of Committal: Used for funerals.

Rite of Christian Initiation of Adults: Used for the rites associated with those of catechetical age who are coming into the Catholic Church.

The Roman Missal: The book that contains all the prayers that the priest uses at Mass. This has also been called the Sacramentary.

Liturgical Objects

Bowls: Bowls are sometimes used instead of patens to hold the consecrated hosts during the distribution of Holy Communion.

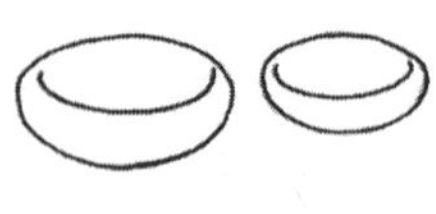

Candle Lighter/Snuffer: A long-handled tool with an extendable wick for lighting candles and a bell-shaped metal part for extinguishing the flames.

Chalice: A cup with a stem that holds the wine before and after consecration.

Ciborium: A container (usually made from metal) with a lid that holds the Blessed Sacrament when it is put in the tabernacle.

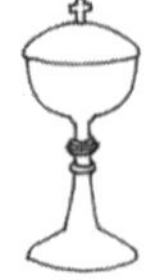

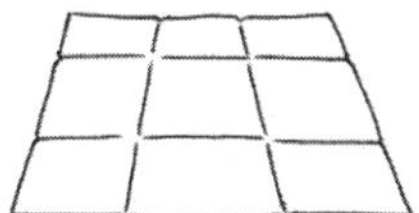

Corporal: A square cloth positioned near the center of the altar on which the vessels holding the consecrated bread and wine are placed.

Cruets: Small pouring containers. One of these is used for the water so a little bit can be added to the wine, and also to pour the water over the priest's hands. Sometimes, if only a little bit of wine will be used, a cruet can be used to contain the wine before it is poured into the chalice.

Cups: A word sometimes used to refer to the chalices into which the consecrated wine is poured for distribution to the people.

Finger Bowl: The small bowl over which the priest holds his hands to catch the water as the altar server pours it over them.

Finger Towel: A small towel that the priest uses to dry his hands.

Holy Oils: Oils that are blessed by the bishop at the Chrism Mass, usually during Holy Week, for distribution to the parishes within the diocese.

> ***Oil of the Catechumens***: Oil that is used for those who are preparing to celebrate the sacrament of baptism.
>
> ***Oil of the Sick:*** Oil that is used to anoint people during the sacrament of the sick.
>
> ***Sacred Chrism:*** Oil that is used at baptism, confirmation, and holy orders. It has a special sweet fragrance.

Holy Water: Water that has been blessed by the priest using a brief prayer.

Holy Water Pot, Bowl, or Bucket: A container, usually with a handle, which holds the holy water so that the presider can use it for sprinkling the people or blessing objects.

Incense Boat: A container holding the incense that will be spooned onto the hot coals for burning. Usually there is a small spoon with the incense boat.

Pall: A covering. During liturgy it is the cloth that is sometimes used to cover the chalice when it is brought to the altar or taken back to the credence table. The large white cloth (white to remind us of baptism) used to cover a casket at funerals is also called a pall.

Paschal Candle: A large candle representing the risen Christ, the light of the world. It is blessed at the Easter Vigil on Holy Saturday and burns at all Masses during the Easter season. It is also used at all funerals and baptisms. Many parishes also burn it at Masses throughout the month of November near a book with the names of those who have died during the past year.

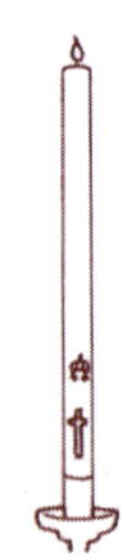

Paten: A plate, usually metal, that holds the consecrated hosts at Mass. Frequently a larger bowl is used to distribute Holy Communion to the assembly.

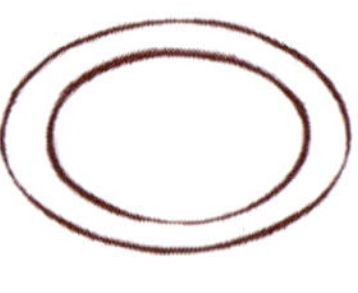

Processional Cross: A cross, usually a crucifix, on a long pole that is used to lead processions.

Purificator: A small piece of white fabric, usually of linen or cotton. The communion ministers use the purificator to wipe the cups or chalices after each person drinks from it.

Sprinkler (aspergillum): A short cylindrical handheld container (usually of metal) for sprinkling holy water.

Thurible (censer): The metal container in which incense is burned. It is hung from long chains so that it can be swung to disperse the incense smoke and aroma.

Thurifer: The person who carries the thurible.

The Liturgical Year

We are used to a year that begins in January, or a school year that begins in August or September. The liturgical year starts about four weeks before Christmas.

Advent: The First Sunday of Advent begins the liturgical year. This is the last Sunday in November or the first Sunday in December. The Advent season is a time of preparation for the celebration of the birth of Jesus at Christmas. There are four Sundays of Advent. The color is violet. The Gloria is not sung to contrast this season with Christmas. At one time Advent was considered a penitential season, but now it is regarded as a season of hopeful anticipation.

Christmas Time: Christmas and the Christmas season follow Advent. The vestment color for Christmas Time is white, although certain feasts during this time may use different colors. During Christmas Time we celebrate the feasts of the Holy Family, the Solemnity of Mary (January 1), the Epiphany, and the Baptism of Jesus. Not all of these feasts occur on Sunday every year. The Baptism of Our Lord is the last day of this season.

Ordinary Time following Christmas: The basic color for this season is green, the color of hope. Various feasts during this time may have their own color, which takes the place of the green. The length of this season varies each year depending on the date of Easter, which is what determines the beginning of Lent.

Lent: Lent begins on Ash Wednesday and includes six Sundays. The color of Lent is violet; the focus of the season is penitential. During this season the Gloria is omitted, and the Alleluia as the Gospel Acclamation before the gospel is replaced by a phrase such as "Praise to you Lord Jesus Christ, King of endless glory." The final Sunday of Lent is Passion or Palm Sunday. Lent continues until the beginning of the Triduum.

Triduum: This begins with the evening Mass of the Lord's Supper on Holy Thursday, includes Good Friday, the Easter Vigil liturgy on the evening of Holy Saturday, and concludes with evening prayer on Easter Sunday. The color for Holy Thursday is white. Good Friday is red. Easter Vigil and Easter Sunday are white.

Easter Time: This season lasts for fifty days from Easter until the evening of Pentecost. It includes the feast of the Ascension. It is a period of joy and celebration. The color of Easter Time is white; the color for Pentecost is red.

Ordinary Time following Easter: This begins the Monday following Pentecost and concludes at the beginning of Advent, when the cycle begins all over again. The first two Sundays in Ordinary Time are the feasts of The Most Holy Trinity and The Most Holy Body and Blood of Christ. The color of these two Sundays is white; the rest of the season is green, except for special feasts.

The Order of Mass

There are four parts of the Mass:

The Introductory Rites
The Liturgy of the Word
The Liturgy of the Eucharist
The Concluding Rites

The Introductory Rites—We Gather

This is the part that gets us into the church building and prepares us to listen to God's word and celebrate The Liturgy of the Eucharist. This preparation actually begins at home as we get ready to come to Mass.

The Introductory Rites include:

The opening song that accompanies the entrance procession

The Sign of the Cross

The greeting by the presider

> This consists of a ritual greeting such as "The Lord be with you" and an optional introduction that the priest may want to give to the liturgy, perhaps explaining the feast of the day or a rite that will take place during the Mass.

The Penitential Act

This can be the Confiteor ("I confess to almighty God …") and/or a "Lord, have mercy" followed by absolution. We acknowledge our need for God's forgiveness and praise God for God's mercy toward us.

The Gloria

This should be sung since it is a hymn of praise, but can be recited instead.

The Collect Prayer

This prayer "collects" the prayers of the assembly and concludes The Introductory Rites.

The Liturgy of the Word—We Listen

This is the part of the Mass where we listen to what God has to say to us through the reading of Scripture. We hear about our church family history and learn about who we are and what our heritage is. We respond in song and prayer.

The Liturgy of the Word includes:

The First Reading

This is usually from the Old Testament. During Easter Time, it is taken from the Acts of the Apostles. It is selected to go with the Gospel reading.

The Responsorial Psalm

This is almost always, with a very few exceptions, taken from the Book of Psalms. Since the psalms were written to be sung, they should be sung during Mass. The psalm, especially the antiphon (the refrain), helps us understand the readings. Each liturgy has its own selected psalm to go with the readings, but it is also possible to use a seasonal psalm that can be used for a number of weeks to capture the focus of the season.

The Second Reading

This reading is from the New Testament. It is usually from one of the letters of Saint Paul or one of the other apostles.

The Gospel Acclamation

For most of the year this is the Alleluia. During Lent the Alleluia is not sung, and instead a different response is used, such as “Praise to you, Lord Jesus Christ, King of endless glory.”

The Gospel

Either the priest or the deacon reads the gospel. These readings are taken from the Gospels of Matthew, Mark, Luke, and John. They are stories from the life of Jesus Christ.

The Homily

The homily also can be done by either the priest or the deacon. Its function is to help us understand how to apply the word that we have heard to our daily lives.

The Profession of Faith (Creed)

This is our response to what we have heard, declaring our faith by reciting the Nicene Creed or the Apostles' Creed. Sometimes a renewal of our Baptismal Promises is used, especially during Easter Time.

The Prayer of the Faithful

As our right and responsibility as baptized Catholics, we continue our response to the readings by praying for the needs of the world and of our community. This prayer concludes The Liturgy of the Word.

The Liturgy of the Eucharist—We Respond

During The Liturgy of the Word we heard about God's goodness to us. Our response is the second half of the Mass in which we give thanks and praise to God for all God has given us. The word "eucharist" means thanksgiving. And this is what we do.

The Liturgy of the Eucharist includes:

The Preparation of the Altar and Gifts

There may be a song or instrumental music at this time. The collection is taken up and the altar is prepared.

The Presentation of the Gifts

The bread and wine are processed up by members of the community. The priest places them on the altar and says blessing prayers of thanksgiving, silently if there is music at this time. He also mixes a little water into the wine.

At this point he washes his hands. If the gifts are incensed, that will take place before he washes his hands. Then he invites all of us to join him in the prayer that follows.

The Eucharistic Prayer

This begins with the Preface and our sung acclamation, the "Holy, Holy, Holy." The Eucharistic Prayer is long and it is said by the priest in our name. We need to pray it along with him, because it is really our prayer that the presider says aloud for us. He asks the Holy Spirit to bless the gifts of bread and wine and to transform them into the Body and Blood of Christ. He recites the words of Christ at the Last Supper and shows us the consecrated bread and wine.

The Memorial Acclamation

This is our chance to respond, usually in song, to acclaim Christ's death and resurrection.

The Eucharistic Prayer continues with offering Christ, the perfect sacrifice, to the Father, and praying for the church, for the world, for those who have died, and for all the church.

The Great Amen

This is our response at the conclusion to the Eucharistic Prayer and it is the way we say our "yes" to all that has been included in the prayer. This is the most important acclamation of the liturgy and should always be sung.

The Communion Rite

In preparation for receiving Holy Communion we say or sing the Our Father and exchange the sign of peace with one another. Usually the servers bring the patens or bowls to the altar at this time. Then we say or sing the "Lamb of God" while the bread is broken and put into the patens or bowls to be distributed to the people.

The priest invites all to come to Holy Communion and receives the consecrated bread and wine himself, after which everyone else processes up to receive. In receiving Christ in Holy Communion we become united ever more closely with Christ and with one another. A communion song is usually sung during this time to express this unity. At the conclusion the priest says the Prayer after Communion, to which we respond "Amen."

The Concluding Rites—We Are Sent Forth

This is the bridge that connects what we have just experienced with our daily lives.

The Concluding Rites include:

Announcements, if there are any

The announcements let us know how we may serve during the week.

The Blessing

The Dismissal and Recessional Song

We are dismissed to live in our daily lives what we have just celebrated at Mass. The final song is not an official part of the liturgy, but can send us out in a joyful manner.

Your Role at Mass

This is a general description of the altar servers' role in the parts of the liturgy. Since there are some differences between one parish and another, the specifics for your parish will have to be learned at the training session.

The Introductory Rites

Your preparation includes choosing what you will wear and refreshing your mind on what you will need to do during the liturgy as an altar server. Once you arrive at church, you may need to sign in, get vested in your alb or cassock and surplice, and help with whatever setup needs to be done. You will also find out if there is anything special or different happening during the liturgy that you will need to know about. You may also be asked to greet people at the church doors to welcome them as they enter. In some parishes the ministers gather before Mass for a brief prayer together.

During the entrance procession you may be carrying the processional cross, a candle, or possibly an incense boat or a censer. If you know the song from memory, you should sing as you process up if that is what the assembly is doing at that time. If you are leading the procession, remember to walk slowly and prayerfully. When you get to the front, usually all line up until the priest arrives and then all bow together. The processional cross bearer does not bow, except perhaps a nod of the head. It is frequently best if the candle bearer not bow either to prevent spilled wax and singed hair. Then all put the cross and candles into their stands and go to their places.

Once in place, you can pick up the hymnal and participate in the song with the rest of the community. When the song is over, make the sign of the cross, respond to the greeting, and participate in the prayers and songs with everyone else. When the priest says, "Let us pray," it is time to bring him whichever book or binder he is using. But don't be surprised if he doesn't say anything right away. He needs to give the people time to respond to the "Let us pray" by forming their own prayers in their hearts. When you hold the book, keep it steady. You can put your hands out flat in front of you like a little shelf to support the book. That will enable the presider to turn pages if necessary. If your fingers are holding the bottom of the pages, he won't be able to do that.

The Liturgy of the Word

You are seated and focus on the person who is reading. This helps to direct everyone else's focus to that person as well. Listen to what God wants to say to you on this day. During the Responsorial Psalm, sing the response with the community. When it is time for the Gospel Alleluia, stand out of respect for the Gospel. It may be that you will use candles and incense at this time depending on the custom in your parish. Following the Gospel all are seated. Some parishes repeat the Gospel Acclamation while the Book of Gospels is placed on a special shelf in sight of the assembly.

Following this all are seated to listen to the homily. It is important to pay attention and look interested. After the homily all stand for the Creed and the Prayer of the Faithful. In some parishes, the presider may wish you to bring him a book or binder for this.

The Liturgy of the Eucharist

During the time of the preparation of the altar and the gifts you will need to prepare the altar. This usually means bringing up a corporal and opening it out on the altar, placing the Roman Missal or whatever book the presider will use for the Eucharistic Prayer, and bringing up the chalice (which may have a pall on it) and the other cups or chalices that may be used, along with the purificators. It may also mean lighting candles at the altar or moving candles from the ambo to the altar.

Once all is ready, you may be seated and sing along if there is a community song. Keep an eye out to see when the presider is ready to go in front of the altar to receive the gifts. He may want you to help carry the gifts and place them for him. You may also need to be ready to take the wine decanter or carafe back to the credence table once the wine has been poured into the cups or chalices.

At some Masses you may need to get the thurible (censer) and incense boat at this time so the presider can incense the gifts and then the people. Once this is done (or following the prayers over the gifts, if no incense is used), bring up the water, finger bowl, and finger towel so he can wash his hands. One of you will pour the water over his hands into the bowl.

During the Eucharistic Prayer, pray along with everyone else and sing the acclamations. If your parish uses the bells during Mass, you will probably be asked to ring them at the Holy, Holy, Holy and at the consecration. You do this when the priest genuflects after he says Christ's words from the Last Supper.

Pray the Our Father and give one another a brief sign of peace. It is now time to bring the patens or bowls up to the altar so the consecrated hosts can be placed in them. When this is completed, say the prayers or sing the songs with everyone else. Then receive communion in the manner you have been instructed. In some parishes you may be wanted to hold a paten for each communicant to prevent the host from dropping.

Following communion you may be expected to "clear the table" and bring the sacred vessels, the book, the corporal, and anything else left on the altar back to the credence table. Once again, the presider will say, "Let us pray," and it is time to bring him the book or binder again.

The Concluding Rites

Listen to the announcements; respond to the blessing and dismissal. On some occasions you may be asked to bring the book or binder up again for a special blessing or prayer over the people. The presider will let you know ahead of time if this is wanted so you can be prepared. When it is time to process out, line up at the foot of the altar with the priest, bow when he bows, and process out in the same order in which you entered, still slowly and reverently. If you can sing the song without a songbook, do so.

Finally, go to the sacristy and assist with any cleanup, then remove your vestments and store them neatly for the next servers to use.

Special Occasions

It is important to arrive early for Mass to find out what special events may occur during the liturgy. It may be a baptism or other special rite. It may be the use of incense. It could be an extra procession. Or it might be a sprinkling rite. Find out what will be expected of you, what will be needed, and be sure to ask any questions so you can be confident in knowing what to do.

Besides the regular Sunday or weekday Masses, you may be called upon to assist with other events, such as weddings or funerals or perhaps baptisms. These also have their special rites requiring the use of holy water and/or incense. Again, be sure to find out what is needed and be clear about what is expected of you. The biggest of special occasions are the liturgies during the Triduum. Holy Thursday, Good Friday, and Easter Vigil Masses are very different from others during the year and will need extra training.

Most parishes have special practices for the altar servers to prepare for these liturgies. It is essential to attend these practices in order to serve at these liturgies. An important part of serving is being able to "think on your feet." Sometimes things don't go as planned. Be prepared to adjust and make everything go smoothly so that the people in the assembly don't know that anything unintended has happened.

Remember that what you do is a prayer.